Whitcomb
9/02
95

W9-AHL-372

Rookie reader

Messy Bessey's
Closet

Written by Patricia and Fredrick McKissack

Illustrated by Dana Regan

Children's Press®
A Division of Scholastic Inc.
New York • Toronto • London • Auckland • Sydney
Mexico City • New Delhi • Hong Kong
Danbury, Connecticut

To Ruth and Martha
and our friends at
Cooperating School District
—P. and F.M.

Reading Consultants
Linda Cornwell
Coordinator of School Quality and Professional Improvement
(Indiana State Teachers Association)

Katharine A. Kane
Education Consultant
(Retired, San Diego County Office of Education
and San Diego State University)

Library of Congress Cataloging-in-Publication Data

McKissack, Pat.
    Messy Bessey's Closet / written by Patricia and Fredrick McKissack ;
illustrated by Dana Regan.
        p. cm. – (Rookie reader)
    Summary: Messy Bessey learns a lesson about sharing when she cleans
out her closet.
    ISBN 0-516-21659-7 (lib. bdg.)   0-516-27081-8 (pbk.)
    [1. Cleanliness—Fiction. 2. Orderliness—Fiction. 3. Sharing—Fiction. 4.
Stories in rhyme.] I. McKissack, Fredrick. II. Regan, Dana, ill. III. Title. IV.
Series.
PZ8.3.M224 Mdc2001
[E]—dc21   00-047370

Look, Messy Bessey!
What do you see?
Your closet, Bessey, is so messy!

See. Open the closet door,
and everything falls on the floor.

Come on now, Messy Bessey.
There is work to do.

Your room is clean and beautiful.
Now clean your closet, too.

9

So Bessey cleaned her closet.
It didn't take too long.

Everything looked wonderful.
But something else was wrong.

13

Messy Bessey looked around.
She really was confused.
What to do with all the things
that she never used?

A ball, a rope,
an old straw hat,

puzzles, games,
and a baseball bat.

A Halloween mask,
and a vampire cape,

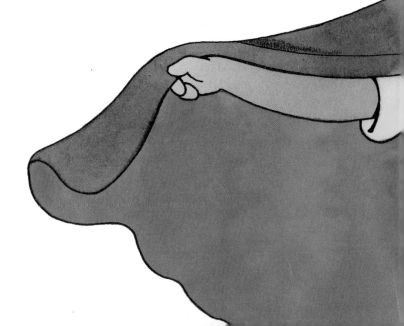

dinosaur posters,
and a funny ape.

Then Messy Bessey thought of a way.
And that is what she did all day—
loving, sharing,

learning, caring,

giving it all away.

Now look what you've done,
Miss Bessey!
We're all so proud of you.

Your room and your *closet*
(just like you) are beautiful
through and through!

Word List (91 words)

a	come	long	straw
all	confused	look	take
an	day	looked	that
and	did	loving	the
ape	didn't	mask	then
are	dinosaur	messy	there
around	do	Miss	things
away	done	never	thought
ball	door	now	through
baseball	else	of	to
bat	everything	old	too
beautiful	falls	on	used
Bessey	floor	open	vampire
but	funny	posters	was
cape	games	proud	way
caring	giving	puzzles	we're
clean	Halloween	really	what
cleaned	hat	room	with
closet	her	rope	wonderful
	is	see	work
	it	sharing	wrong
	just	she	you
	learning	so	you've
	like	something	your

About the Authors

Patricia and Fredrick McKissack are freelance writers and editors, living in St. Louis County, Missouri. Their awards as authors include the Coretta Scott King Award, the Jane Addams Peace Award, the Newbery Honor, and the 1998 Regina Medal from the Catholic Library Association. The McKissacks have also written *Messy Bessey, Messy Bessey and the Birthday Overnight, Messy Bessey's Family Reunion, Messy Bessey's Garden, Messy Bessey's Holidays,* and *Messy Bessey's School Desk* in the Rookie Reader series.

About the Illustrator

Dana Regan was born and raised in northern Wisconsin. She migrated south to Washington University in St. Louis, and eventually to Kansas City, Missouri, where she now lives with her husband, Dan, and her sons, Joe and Tommy.